FOR AGES 5-7
BRILLIANT IDEAS FOR
TIMES TABLES
Practice

by Molly Potter

ANDREW BRODIE
AN IMPRINT OF BLOOMSBURY
LONDON NEW DELHI   NEW YORK   SYDNEY

First published 2012 by Andrew Brodie
an imprint of Bloomsbury Publishing Plc
50 Bedford Square
London WC1B 3DP
ISBN 9781408181300

Text © Molly Potter 2012
Illustrations © Mike Phillips/Beehive Illustration

Printed and bound by CPI Group (UK) Ltd, Croydon CR0 4YY

13 5 7 9 10 8 6 4 2

This book is produced using paper that is made from wood grown in
managed, sustainable forests. It is natural, renewable and recyclable.
The logging and manufacturing processes conform to the environmental
regulations of the country of origin.

To see our full range of titles visit www.bloomsbury.com

Contents

Introduction 4

2 times table poster 5
Join the sum to its answer 7
Colour match 8
Which is the right answer? 9
Two times table clown 10
How do these aliens feel? 11
Complete the picture 12
Whose sum is it? 13
Hidden numbers 14
Sum search 15
Answer hunt 16

5 times table poster 17
Join the sum to its answer 19
Colour match 20
Counting in fives 21
Monster pet shop 22
Hidden picture 23
Find the wrong answers 24
What is the speed limit? 25
Dot to dot in fives 26
Treasure Island 27

10 times table poster 28
Join the sum to its answer 30
Colour match 31
Find the wrong answers 32
Multiply by ten 33
Who has the most balloons? 34
It's tops 35
Find out about Trogg 36
Find the answers 37
Which is the right answer? 38

2, 5 and 10 times tables
This is the answer: what is the question? 39
Multiply by? 40
What's hidden in the picture? 41
Fill the flowers 42
What is his job? 43
Test a friend 44
Which is bigger? 45
Dot to dot 46
Monster maths 47
Who won the race? 48

3 times table poster 49
Colour match 51
Find out what they said 52
What do they eat? 53
Journey to the answer 54
Label with sums 55
Complete the picture 56
How many triangles? 57
Monster meal 58
This is the answer: what is the question? 59
Race! 60

Answers 61

Introduction

THIS BOOK

This book provides a selection of activities to help pupils not only to learn their tables, but also to feel more positive about them. It includes a mix of straight forward and more involved and creative activities to encourage pupils to associate tables with fun while they learn them for life.

HOW TO USE THIS SERIES

This book and the others in the series support the learning of each multiplication table starting with a poster that can be used to introduce each specific table. This can be coloured in and used by the pupils at home to aid their learning. The easier activities start each section dedicated to a particular table. Many of these can be used more than once to teach and revisit each table – especially the revision activities. Some more difficult sheets could be enlarged to A3 and pupils can work together to solve the challenges.

NEW APPROACHES TO LEARNING

Why not decide to make this the year that all of your class learn their tables once and for all? What a gift to give them! With a little extra effort this is quite possible. Here are some suggestions to help you:

- *Tackle the motivation to learn multiplication tables and find the best ways to learn them*
Discuss why times tables are in the curriculum and how knowing them not only makes their school maths career much easier but stands them in good stead for the future. For example, as an adult they might need to find out the cost of several items of the same price, the amount needed for a meal, how to calculate how many days there are in a number of weeks and so on.

Have a discussion about learning tables – what makes it hard, what stops some people from learning them? Ask pupils to discuss in pairs what they believe would help them to learn their multiplication tables or if they have already mastered them – what did they do? Ask pupils to write their ideas down on sticky notes and stick them onto a large sheet of paper (for younger children, just pool your ideas). Discuss the ideas they create and make a plan to help your class learn their tables.

- *Create a 'Table of the week' each week*
Choose one of the more difficult tables to focus on each week. Display that table with its answer and its inverse sum boldly in the classroom. For example $8 \times 7 = 56$ and $7 \times 8 = 56$. If possible, include an interesting fact about the answer or a picture that relates to the sum or answer.

- *List difficult tables*
Some tables are definitely more difficult to remember than others. Create a 'tricky tables' poster. Pupils could agree on a mark out of ten for the difficulty of each sum.

- *Have individual table cards for pupils*
Create differentiated lists of multiplication tables with three columns beside each sum. Pupils can colour inside the three columns next to each table red (do not know it), then add amber (nearly know it) and finally green (always get it right). Allow pupils time to look at this card regularly to review their own learning and try to learn those they have not yet mastered.

- *Play tables games*
Use games such as those included in these books (especially 9–11) regularly to revise the tables in an entertaining way.

A whole-class game that can be used to revise tables is 'winner stays on'. First choose two pupils to stand up. Next ask a times table question. The first pupil to shout out the answer stays standing, the other pupil sits down. Another pupil is asked to stand, another sum issued and again the first person to shout the answer is the winner who then stays on and so on.

- *Create a times tables test and award*
To achieve this award any pupil has to correctly answer 20 random multiplication table questions of those that have been covered in your class. If they succeed they can be issued the award (a badge, a certificate or a significant number of 'merits' from the existing classroom reward system). Explain to the class that they can request to take the tables test at any point in the year to try and achieve the award to aid continuous motivation to learn.

The 2 x Table

1 x 2 = 2

I have one lot of two eyes which makes two eyes only. Gosh I am clever.

That's a simple square number.

2 x 2 = 4

3 x 2 = 6

I see this when I look at an ant's legs.

4 x 2 = 8

This one is so easy. I say it over and over and it always sends me to sleep.

Two jazz hands of five fingers makes ten jazz fingers.

5 x 2 = 10

This one is the story of my legs.

6 x 2 = 12

Join the sum to its answer

Name _____ **Date** _____

Use colouring pencils to join each sum to its answer. One has been done for you.

8

1 x 2

6 x 2

12

4 x 2

10

2

2 x 2

14

5 x 2

6

4

18

7 x 2

3 x 2

9 x 2

8

4 x 2

20

10 x 2

Now answer these sums

2 x 2 = ☐	9 x 2 = ☐	2 x 9 = ☐
4 x 2 = ☐	2 x 10 = ☐	2 x 4 = ☐
6 x 2 = ☐	2 x 6 = ☐	2 x 8 = ☐
7 x 2 = ☐	2 x 3 = ☐	2 x 11 = ☐
8 x 2 = ☐	2 x 5 = ☐	2 x 7 = ☐

Colour match

Name _____ **Date** _____

Colour the sums in the box different colours. For example 1 x 2 could be black and 2 x 2 could be green etc. Now find the answers and colour them to match

22   4   12

2   16   24

8   16

10   18   4

14   4

6   22   14

12   18   8

2   12

18   8   16

8

4   6   16

10   24   12

Which is the right answer?

x2   **Name** _____   **Date** _____

Choose the correct answer for each sum and circle it.

1 x 2 =   1   4   2   8   0

2 x 1 =   1   2   4   20

2 x 2 =   4   16   8   10

2 x 4 =   4   10   8   3

3 x 2 =   2   6   4   10   8

2 x 8 =   10   16   8   4

4 x 2 =   6   4   12   8   2

2 x 9 =   18   20   10   8

5 x 2 =   5   10   20   8

2 x 6 =   6   4   18   8   12

6 x 2 =   6   10   8   12   20

2 x 5 =   5   4   20   10

7 x 2 =   10   12   14   8   16

5 x 2 =   6   10   8   20

8 x 2 =   0   10   14   4   16

2 x 7 =   10   12   14   16

9 x 2 =   6   14   18   22

2 x 2 =   0   2   4   6   1

10 x 2 =   22   20   14   10   11

2 x 3 =   6   4   10   22

11 x 2 =   14   18   20   22   8

2 x 11 =   22   20   10   11

12 x 2 =   24   22   14   10   18

2 x 12 =   14   12   24   8

Two times table clown

Name _____   **Date** _____

The answers to these sums are found in this picture. Match the colours to the answers to colour in the clown.

1 x 2 = black
2 x 2 = pink
3 x 2 = red
4 x 2 = green
5 x 2 = yellow
6 x 2 = orange
7 x 2 = purple
8 x 2 = blue
9 x 2 = brown
10 x 2 = white

How do these aliens feel?

Name _____ **Date** _____

Answer each sum to find the correct mouth for each alien or monster and find out how they felt about what happened.

Mouths

2	╱
4	●
6	◗
8	‿
10	⌣ (with teeth)
12	—
14	∿
16	◡ (tongue)
18	▰◆▰
20	╱

Mr Trog just trod on a horse

2 x 10

Zog just ate some worms

2 x 5

Chuzzy just looked in a mirror

2 x 2

Wozz just drank some lemonade

2 x 4

Ted just got a tree stuck up his nose

2 x 3

Shrig just crashed her spaceship

2 x 7

Grog just smelled a rose

2 x 8

Plox just tripped over an elephant

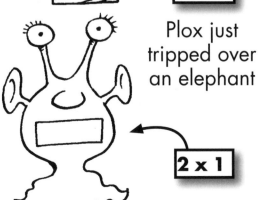

2 x 1

Yetto is on a ghost train

2 x 9

Trevor's ear just fell off

2 x 6

Complete the picture

Name _____ **Date** _____

Use the answers to these sums to complete the picture of this monster.

(**2 x 7 wavy hairs on head**)

(**2 x 2 eyes**)

(**2 x 1 big round ears**)

**2 x 9 spots
on face**

**2 x 4 arms and hands
2 x 8 fingers in total**

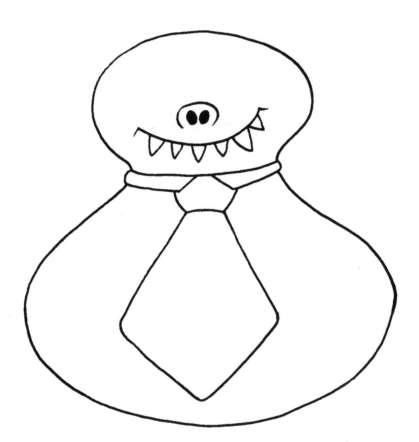

**2 x 10 dots
on his tie**

**2 x 3 legs and feet
2 x 6 toes in total**

(**2 x 5 flowers in his hand**)

Whose sum is it?

Name _____ **Date** _____

Each character is holding a sum in the two times table. Work out which sum belongs to each character. There are lots of clues in the pictures of each character.

Once you have written the sum on the character's card, cross it off from the list below. You should use up all the sums.

$$1 \times 2 \qquad 9 \times 2 \qquad 2 \times 2 \qquad 7 \times 2 \qquad 3 \times 2 \qquad 5 \times 2$$

Hidden numbers

Name _____ **Date** _____

Look for the answers to these sums in the picture. Use the boxes to keep a tally of the number of times you find the answers.

1 x 2

2 x 2

3 x 2

10 x 2

4 x 2

9 x 2

5 x 2

8 x 2

7 x 2

6 x 2

Brilliant Ideas for Times Tables 5–7 © Molly Potter 2012

Sum search

Name _____ **Date** _____

In this box you can find several sums in the two times table by using a ruler. One sum (2 x 4 = 8) has been done for you. See if you can find all the others. The first number in each sum has been circled. When you have found them all, every number and symbol will be crossed out.

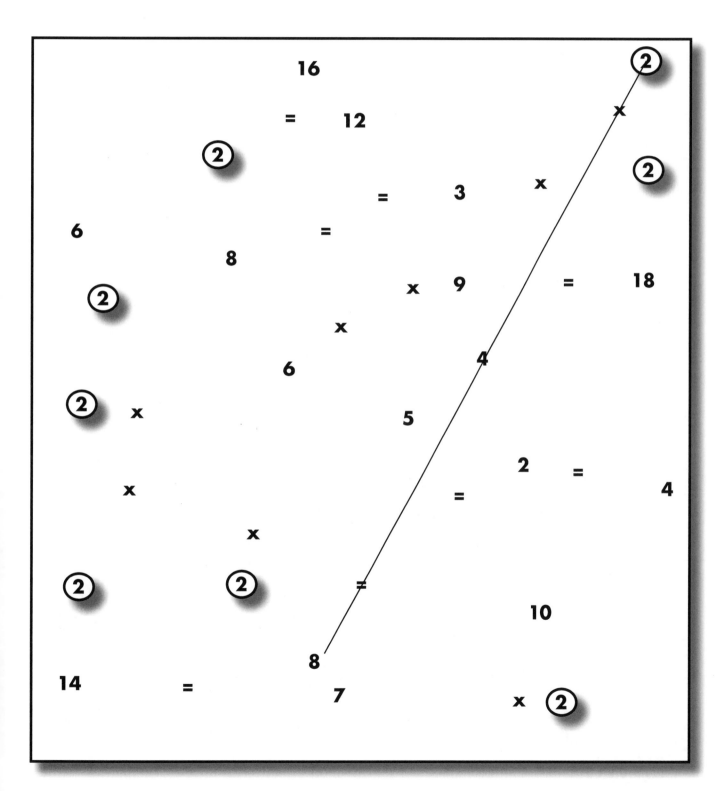

Answer hunt

Name _____ **Date** _____

Select the right answer for each question.

Question		Choose the answer
How many clouds are there?		2 x 3 or 2 x 4
How many hairs come out of the alien's ears?		2 x 9 or 2 x 6
How many spiky trees are there?		2 x 2 or 2 x 3
How many fruits are there in the fruit bush?		2 x 9 or 2 x 10

Question		Choose the answer
How many teeth has the alien?		2 x 6 or 2 x 7
How many wheels on the alien's car?		2 x 5 or 2 x 4
How many eyes has the alien?		2 x 2 or 2 x 3
How many spots on the alien's nose?		2 x 6 or 2 x 7

The 5 x Table

Join the sum to its answer

Name _____ **Date** _____

Use colouring pencils to join each sum to its answer. One has been done for you.

Now answer these sums.

5 x 5 = ☐	3 x 5 = ☐	5 x 3 = ☐
2 x 5 = ☐	10 x 5 = ☐	1 x 5 = ☐
5 x 2 = ☐	5 x 1 = ☐	5 x 5 = ☐
4 x 5 = ☐	5 x 2 = ☐	7 x 5 = ☐
5 x 6 = ☐	6 x 5 = ☐	5 x 4 = ☐

Colour match

Name _____ **Date** _____

Colour the sums in the box different colours. For example 1 x 5 could be black and 2 x 5 could be green etc. Now find the answers and colour them to match.

Counting in fives

x5 **Name** _____ **Date** _____

Counting in fives is easy once you get into the swing of it. Fill in the missing numbers in each of these lists of the five times table.

5, 10, _____, 20, 25, 30, _____, 40, 45, _____

5, 10, 15, _____, 25, _____, 35, 40, _____, 50

5, 10, 15, _____, _____, 30, 35, _____, _____, 50

5, _____, 15, _____, 25, _____, 35, _____, 45, _____

_____, 10, _____, 20, _____, 30, _____, 40, _____, 50

_____, 10, _____, _____, _____, 30, _____, _____, 45, _____

_____, _____, _____, _____, _____, _____, _____, _____,
50, _____, _____, _____

5, _____

See if you can count up to 100 in fives.

Brilliant Ideas for Times Tables 5–7 © Molly Potter 2012   **21**

Monster pet shop

Name _____   **Date** _____

These are all pets found in a monster pet shop. Which one do you think you would like as your pet? Now use the answers to the sums to find out what each of the pets eat.

5	10	15	20	25	30	35	40	45	50
bricks	sweets	money	giraffes	doors	litter	cars	daffodils	mud	people

A fliggy
I eat _____
2 x 5

A snoodle
I eat _____   5 x 5

A gruff
I eat _____
3 x 5

A chirt
I eat
_____
8 x 5

A groar
I eat _____
7 x 5

A jick
I eat _____
6 x 5

A kudgy
I eat _____
10 x 5

An elepop
I eat _____
4 x 5

A stug
I eat _____
9 x 5

A cutop
I eat _____
1 x 5

Hidden picture

Name _____   **Date** _____

Colour in the shapes that contain a number in the five times table and you will see a picture. Can you see what it is?

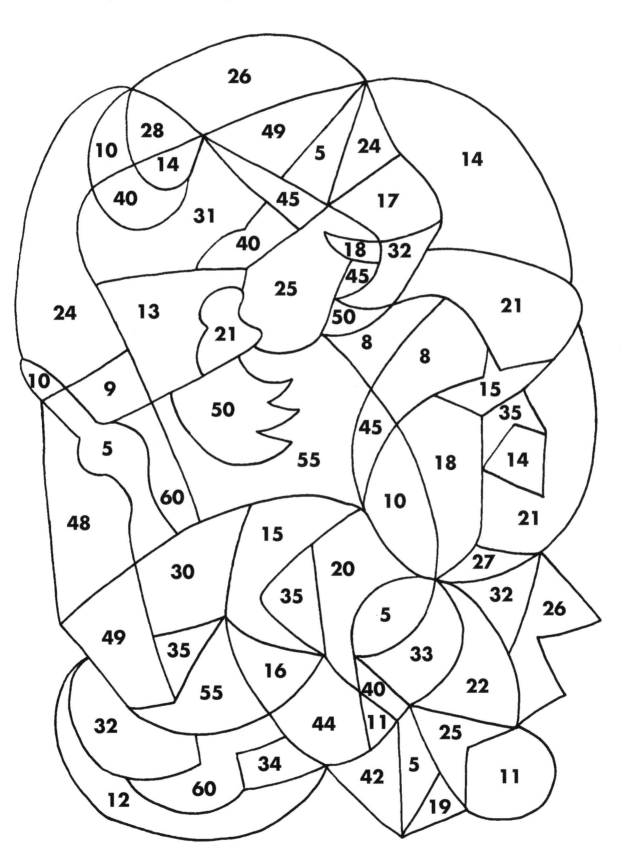

Find the wrong answers

Name _____ **Date** _____

In each blob, colour in the circles with the wrong answers to leave the right answer. One has been done for you.

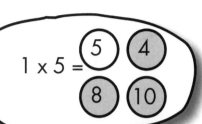

$1 \times 5 =$ (5) (4) (8) (10)

$8 \times 5 =$ (40) (30) (20) (45)

$5 \times 7 =$ (30) (49) (40) (35)

$5 \times 6 =$ (36) (15) (30) (25)

$5 \times 5 =$ (20) (15) (25) (28)

$5 \times 2 =$ (15) (5) (10) (12)

$5 \times 3 =$ (10) (12) (15) (18)

$10 \times 5 =$ (10) (50) (25) (55)

$3 \times 5 =$ (10) (5) (20) (15)

$9 \times 5 =$ (18) (50) (40) (45)

$5 \times 4 =$ (16) (20) (25) (18)

$4 \times 5 =$ (10) (25) (20) (16)

What is the speed limit?

Answer the sums to find out the speed limit for each road sign.

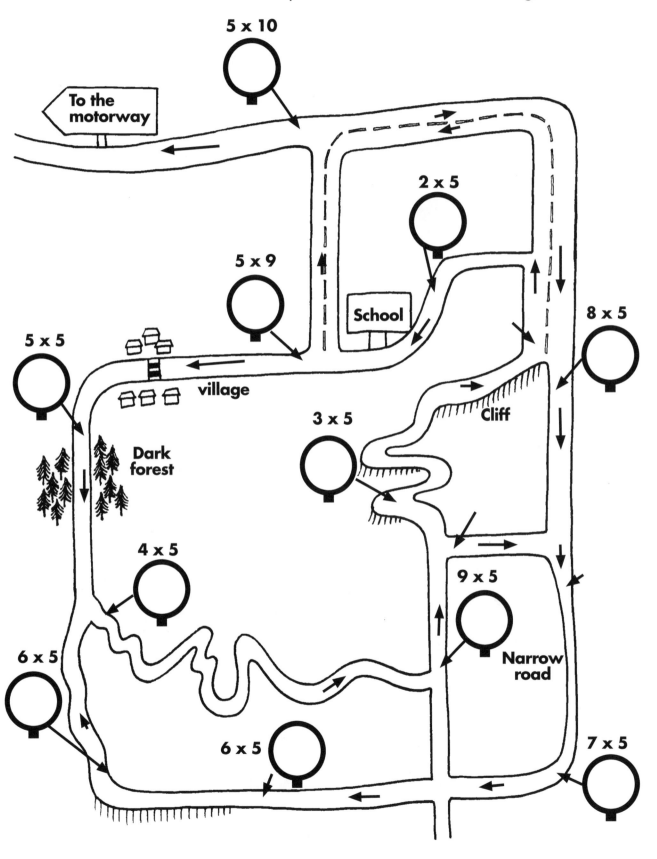

Do you think the speed limits are right?

Dot to dot in fives

Name _____ **Date** _____

Complete this dot to dot by counting in fives. First join the plain numbers that go up in fives: 5, 10, 15 etc. Then the numbers in squares that go up in fives: 5, 10, 15 etc. (numbers in squares). And lastly, join the circled numbers that go up in fives: 5, 10, 15 etc. (numbers in circles).

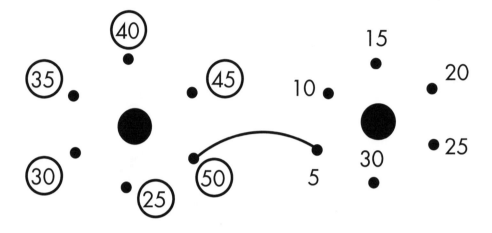

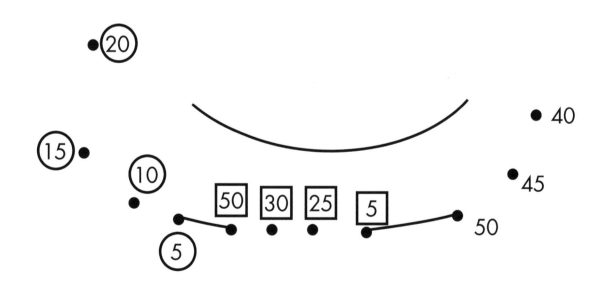

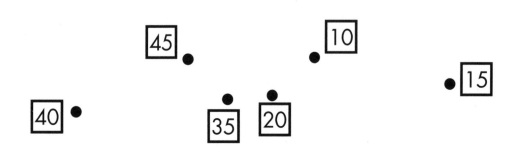

Treasure Island

Name _____   **Date** _____

There is treasure hidden on this island. Pirates were looking for it but they did not find it. They travelled to all the numbers shown on this map. They went from number to number in a straight line. They left this piece of paper as a clue to the route they took. Draw lines on the map to show the route the pirates took and see if you can work out where the treasure is before the pirates do.

- 1 x 5 =
- 10 x 5 =
- 5 x 5 =
- 3 x 5 =
- 7 x 5 =
- 4 x 5 =
- 2 x 5 =
- 6 x 5 =
- 8 x 5 =
- 9 x 5 =
- 1 x 5 =

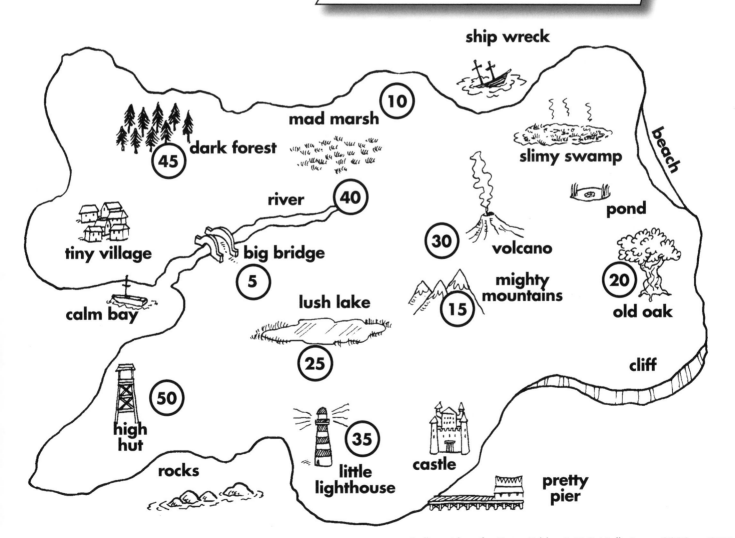

The 10 x Table

1 x 10 = 10

Even I can do this one!

That's all my fingers and all my toes!

I eat 30 lollipops a day. They call me lollipop man!

2 x 10 = 20

Today's lollipops

3 x 10 = 30

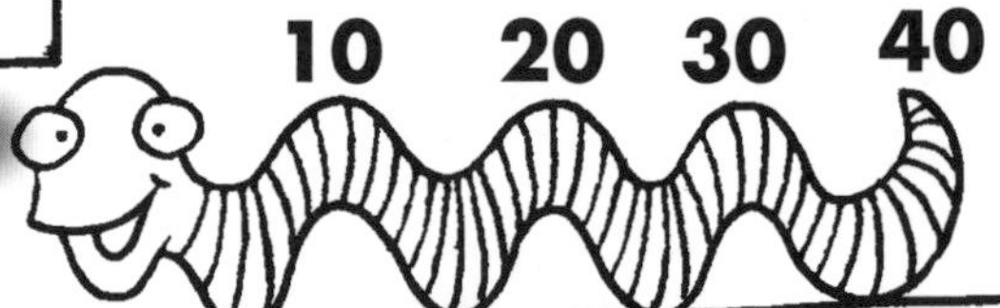

10   20   30   40

I think I can see a pattern.

4 x 10 = 40

Even I can do this one!

I have 60 spots on the front of my trousers, oh, and six legs!

5 x 10 = 50

6 x 10 = 60

Join the sum to its answer

Name _____   **Date** _____

Use colouring pencils to join each sum to its answer. One has been done for you.

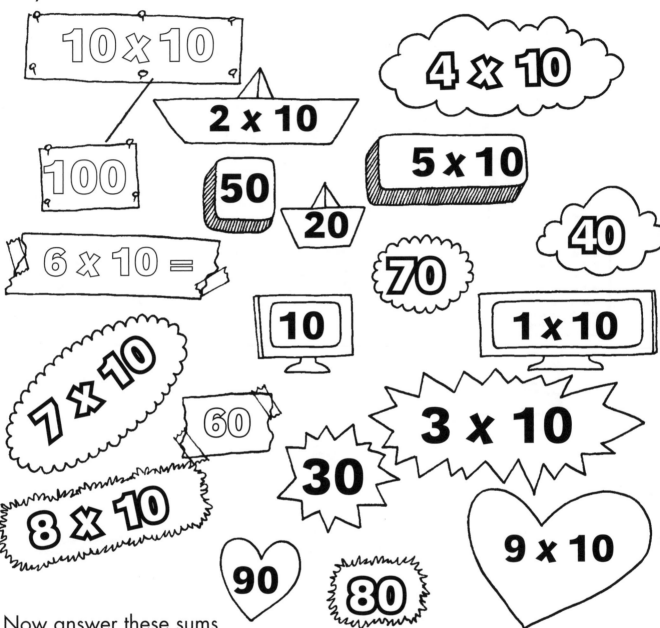

Now answer these sums.

4 x 10 = ☐	10 x 4 = ☐	10 x 9 = ☐
10 x 6 = ☐	10 x 1 = ☐	8 x 10 = ☐
10 x 10 = ☐	10 x 2 = ☐	9 x 10 = ☐
10 x 5 = ☐	6 x 10 = ☐	10 x 7 = ☐
7 x 10 = ☐	10 x 3 = ☐	10 x 10 = ☐

Activity Sheet 22

Colour match

x10

Name ______________________ **Date** ________________

Colour the sums in the box different colours. For example 1 x 10 could be black and 2 x 10 could be green etc. Now find the answers and colour them to match.

1 x 10
2 x 10
3 x 10
4 x 10
5 x 10
6 x 10
7 x 10
8 x 10
9 x 10
10 x 10
11 x 10
12 x 10

70 110
60 90
50
120 120
80
70 30 50
40 100
90 10 60
30 40 100
20 120
80 110 10

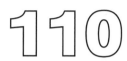

x10

Find the wrong answers

Name _____ **Date** _____

Answer the sum in each of these shapes and then colour in the wrong numbers black. One has been done for you. When you have finished, a picture should appear (especially if you hold the page away from you to get a better look).

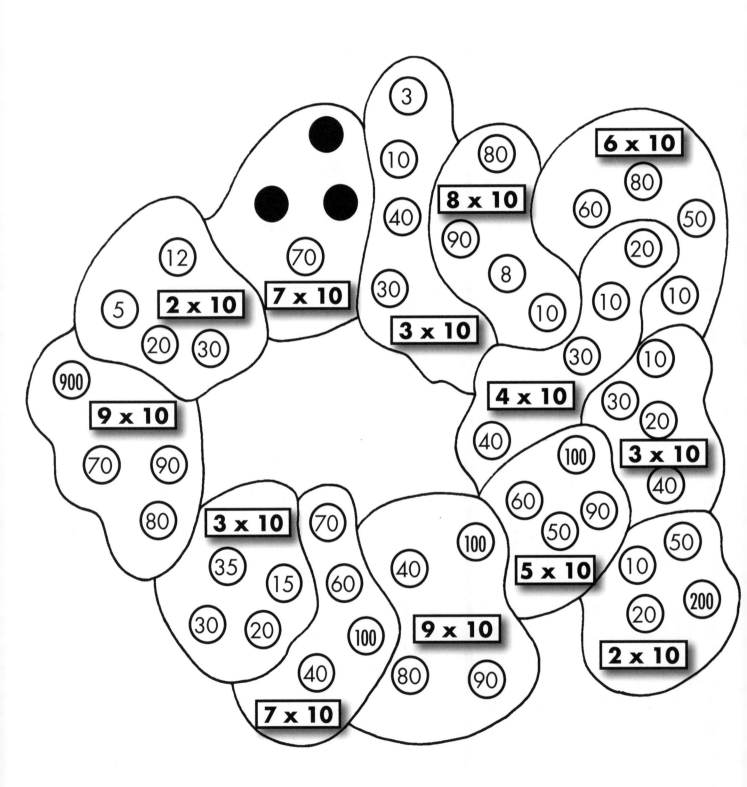

Multiply by ten

Name _____ **Date** _____

Multiply all these numbers by ten and put the answer in the space below them. One has been done for you.

x 10

7	2	5	4	1	9	8	3	6	10
				10					

x 10

10	7	2	8	5	1	9	6	4	3

x 10

3	1	4	8	10	9	5	2	7	6

x 10

1	5	8	2	6	9	3	7	10	4

Who has the most balloons?

x10

Name _____ **Date** _____

Join the hands with the sums to the balloons with the answers. Which hand has the most balloons?

It's tops

Name _____ **Date** _____

Draw the correct top onto each character by matching the sum to its answer.

3 x10

8 x10

4 x10

9 x10

6 x10

1 x10

10 x10

2 x10

5 x10

7 x10

10	
20	
30	
40	
50	
60	
70	
80	
90	
100	

Find out about Trogg

Name _____   **Date** _____

This is Trogg. Find out some information about her by cracking the code.

0	10	20	30	40	50	60	70	80	90	100
s	o	c	t	r	u	g	e	a	h	l

What does Trogg eat?   _____ _____ _____ _____ _____
(0 x 10) (10 x 10) (5 x 10) (6 x 10) (0 x 10)

What does Trogg hate?

_____ _____ _____ _____ _____ _____
(3 x 10) (4 x 10) (1 x 10) (10 x 10) (10 x 10) (0 x 10)

What does Trogg squash?   _____ _____ _____ _____
(2 x 10) (8 x 10) (4 x 10) (0 x 10)

What does Trogg pick her nose with?

_____ _____ _____ _____ _____
(3 x 10) (4 x 10) (7 x 10) (7 x 10) (0 x 10)

What does Trogg smell of?

_____ _____ _____ _____ _____ _____
(2 x 10) (9 x 10) (7 x 10) (7 x 10) (0 x 10) (7 x 10)

Find the answers

In this picture see how many times you can find the answers to the sums in the ten times table. When you find an answer, label it with its sum. One has been done for you. The sums you need are:

1 x 10   2 x 10   3 x 10   4 x 10   5 x 10
6 x 10   7 x 10   8 x 10   9 x 10   10 x 10

You can find each answer more than once.

1 x 10

Which is the right answer?

x10   **Name** _____   **Date** _____

Choose the correct answer for each sum and circle it.

1 x 10 = 1   10   15   20   100   40

10 x 1 = 40   70   65   50   15   30   10

2 x 10 = 20   15   10   100   30   0

10 x 4 = 60   40   10   30   35

3 x 10 = 600   40   300   35   30

10 x 8 = 100   20   70   80   40

4 x 10 = 15   30   20   10   40   80

10 x 9 = 45   80   70   90   100   0

5 x 10 = 55   20   40   100   20   50

10 x 6 = 6   30   10   80   60   20

6 x 10 = 20   40   60   15   30   80

10 x 5 = 5   60   40   100   50

7 x 10 = 90   50   70   20   700   25

10 x 2 = 30   10   40   20   100

8 x 10 = 80   50   40   60   70   100   30

10 x 7 = 60   80   30   70   100

9 x 10 = 70   20   100   30   90

10 x 10 = 90   80   50   100   60   0

10 x 10 = 80   40   20   90   100

10 x 3 = 90   30   0   10   20

This is the answer: what is the question?

Name _____ **Date** _____

Circle the sum on each line that matches the answers on the left.

18	2 x 6	5 x 3	10 x 2	2 x 9
15	3 x 3	4 x 3	5 x 3	6 x 3
30	8 x 3	5 x 3	2 x 10	10 x 3
14	2 x 6	5 x 3	2 x 7	2 x 10
12	2 x 6	5 x 3	1 x 10	2 x 5
20	10 x 3	5 x 5	10 x 2	5 x 3
8	2 x 6	10 x 1	5 x 2	2 x 4
16	5 x 3	2 x 7	2 x 8	5 x 4
6	2 x 3	1 x 5	2 x 2	10 x 1
4	1 x 1	1 x 2	2 x 2	4 x 2
25	4 x 5	5 x 3	6 x 5	5 x 5
10	2 x 4	2 x 5	5 x 3	2 x 10
30	5 x 6	7 x 5	8 x 5	10 x 2
45	4 x 5	5 x 5	4 x 10	9 x 5
40	10 x 2	5 x 8	4 x 2	5 x 9

Name _____   **Date** _____

Multiply these numbers by the number above and put the answer in the space below them. One has been done for you.

x 10

7	2	5	4	1	9	8	3	6	10
70									

x 2

10	7	2	8	5	1	9	6	4	3

x 5

3	1	4	8	10	9	5	2	7	6

x 2

1	5	8	2	6	9	3	7	10	4

x 5

8	4	9	10	7	2	3	5	6	1

What's hidden in the picture?

x2 x5 x10

Name _____ **Date** _____

Colour in the shapes that hold the answers to the sums below and see what shape is made.

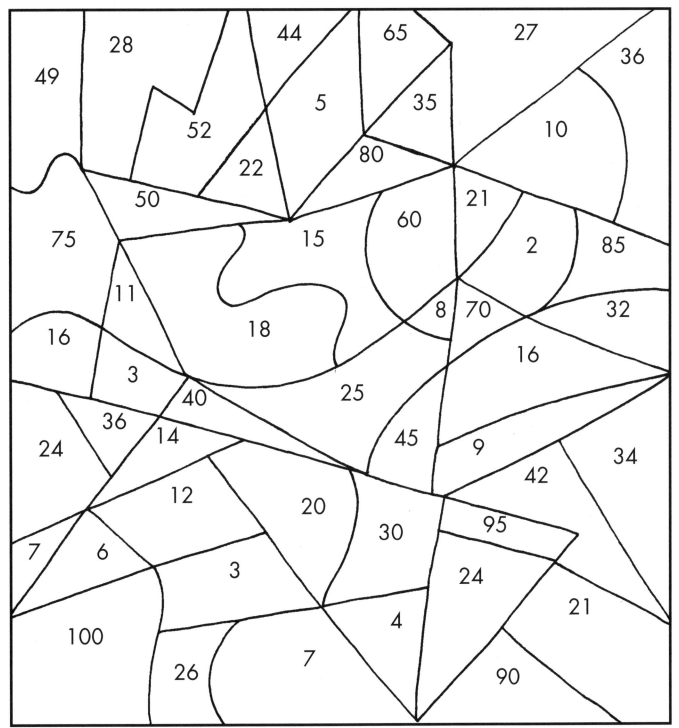

5 x 10 =	8 x 5 =	7 x 5 =	2 x 2 =
2 x 9 =	4 x 5 =	8 x 10 =	7 x 10 =
9 x 5 =	6 x 10 =	3 x 5 =	5 x 5 =
2 x 3 =	2 x 6 =	2 x 7 =	2 x 4 =

Fill the flowers

Name _____ **Date** _____

Find the numbers that match the sums and put them into the
correct flower. Draw a line from the sum to the petal with its answer.
Cross the sums off as you match them. One has been done for you.

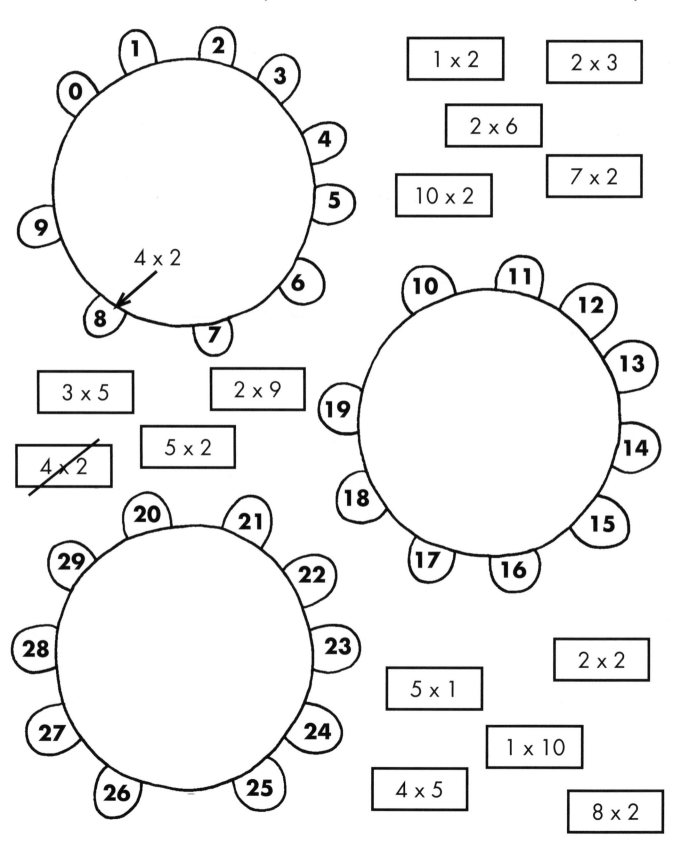

1 x 2   2 x 3

2 x 6

10 x 2   7 x 2

4 x 2

3 x 5   2 x 9

5 x 2

4 x 2

2 x 2

5 x 1

1 x 10

4 x 5

8 x 2

What is his job?

Name _____   **Date** _____

Klonk is a rather odd creature. He is also quite dangerous. Find out how he got his name and why he is dangerous by cracking the code.

a	b	c	d	e	f	g	h	i	j	k	l	m
15	10	25	21	20	24	35	2	14	8	40	18	16

n	o	p	q	r	s	t	u	v	w	x	y	z
80	6	5	28	70	4	90	32	12	50	45	30	100

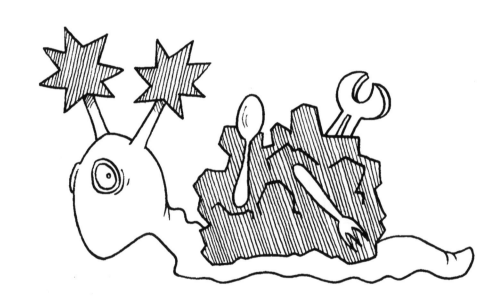

___   ___
1 x 2   4 x 5

___   ___
2 x 7   2 x 2

___
3 x 5

___   ___   ___   ___   ___   ___
7 x 10   2 x 10   5 x 3   2 x 9   9 x 2   5 x 6

___   ___   ___   ___   ___   ___
2x2   10 x 9   10 x 7   2 x 3   8 x 10   7 x 5

___   ___   ___   ___   ___   ___
4x4   3 x 5   5 x 7   8 x 10   10 x 2   9 x 10

Test a friend

x2
x5
x10

Name _____ **Date** _____

Cut these cards out and find a partner. Ask your partner the sum on the card and see how many they can answer before making a mistake. The answers are at the bottom of the cards – so be careful not to let your partner see them. Keep their score. Now give your friend the cards and see how many you can answer before you make a mistake.

2 x 9 18	4 x 10 40	10 x 10 100	6 x 10 60
8 x 2 16	10 x 3 30	2 x 6 12	5 x 3 15
8 x 10 80	5 x 5 25	5 x 4 20	4 x 2 8
7 x 5 35	2 x 2 4	9 x 5 45	2 x 9 18
9 x 10 90	10 x 2 20	2 x 3 6	5 x 8 40
5 x 2 10	5 x 6 30	7 x 10 70	2 x 7 14

Brilliant Ideas for Times Tables 5–7 © Molly Potter 2012

Which is bigger?

Name _____ **Date** _____

For each pair of sums, work out which one gives the bigger number. If the answers come to the same amount, ring both answers. The first one has been done for you.

⑴ (4 x 2) or 1 x 5

⑵ 2 x 5 or 4 x 2

⑶ 2 x 2 or 1 x 5

⑷ 7 x 2 or 3 x 5

⑸ 1 x 10 or 2 x 6

⑹ 4 x 2 or 2 x 5

⑺ 3 x 5 or 8 x 2

⑻ 3 x 10 or 7 x 5

⑼ 2 x 9 or 4 x 5

⑽ 2 x 10 or 5 x 5

⑾ 2 x 3 or 1 x 5

⑿ 3 x 5 or 7 x 2

⒀ 5 x 6 or 3 x 10

⒁ 9 x 2 or 3 x 5

⒂ 2 x 4 or 5 x 2

⒃ 3 x 5 or 2 x 6

⒄ 4 x 10 or 8 x 5

⒅ 5 x 5 or 2 x 10

⒆ 1 x 10 or 2 x 5

⒇ 3 x 5 or 2 x 10

Dot to dot

Name _____ **Date** _____

This is a dot to dot with a difference. Work out all the sums and then join the numbers from the smallest to the biggest to make a picture. What can you see?

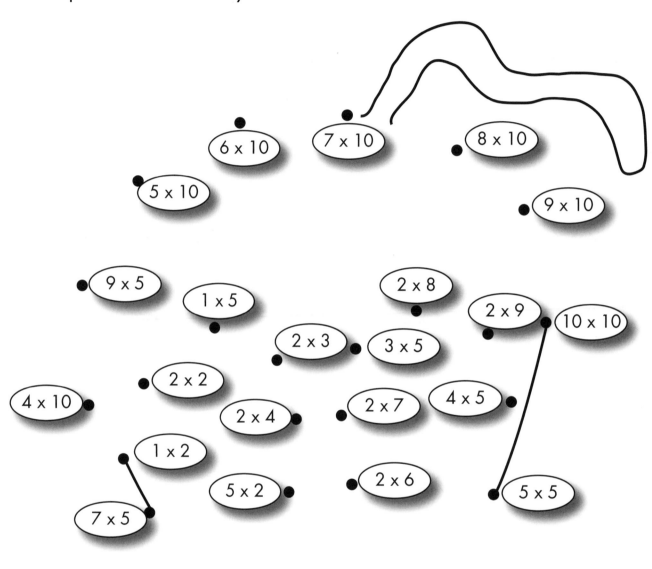

6 x 10

7 x 10

8 x 10

5 x 10

9 x 10

9 x 5

2 x 8

1 x 5

2 x 9

10 x 10

2 x 3

3 x 5

2 x 2

4 x 10

2 x 7

4 x 5

2 x 4

1 x 2

2 x 6

5 x 5

5 x 2

7 x 5

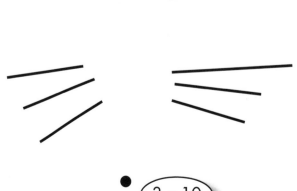

3 x 10

Brilliant Ideas for Times Tables 5–7 © Molly Potter 2012

Monster maths

Name _____   **Date** _____

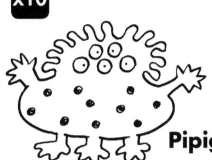  

Pipig   **Grot**   **Krell**

If Pipig, Grot and Krell always look exactly the same, how many...

(1) Eyes would five Pipig have?

Example 5 x 5 = 25 _____

(2) Wheels would two Krell have?

_____

(3) Spots would ten Pipig have?

_____

(4) Teeth would two Grot have?

_____

(5) Legs would five Pipig have?

_____

(6) Ears would ten Grot have?

_____

(7) Legs would five Grot have?

(8) Spots would seven Pipig have?

_____

(9) Eyes would ten Pipig have?

_____

(10) Teeth would five Grot have?

_____

(11) Legs would ten Pipig have?

_____

(12) Wheels would five Krell have?

_____

(13) Hands would six Pipig have?

_____

(14) Eyes would nine Pipig have?

_____

Who won the race?

x2
x5
x10
x3

Name _____ **Date** _____

Work out these sums and put a tick on the table to match the answers. Each time the answer comes up it scores a point. Which number scores the most and wins the race? The first sum has been done for you. Make sure you cross out each sum after you have done it.

4	4					
5						
6						
8						
9						
10						
12						
15						
16						
18						
20						
21						
24						
25						
27						
30						
35						
40						
45						
50						

~~1 x 4~~ | 6 x 5 | 6 x 2

7 x 3 | 4 x 5 | 2 x 3

9 x 2 | 6 x 3 | 3 x 9

3 x 4 | 5 x 5 | 2 x 9

5 x 3 | 2 x 8 | 5 x 1

3 x 3 | 3 x 8 | 5 x 5

6 x 2 | 5 x 10 | 3 x 4

2 x 5 | 9 x 5 | 5 x 4

8 x 3 | 7 x 5 | 5 x 5

3 x 5 | 2 x 10 | 1 x 5

5 x 6 | 3 x 6 | 9 x 3

5 x 9 | 5 x 7 | 4 x 4 | 2 x 2 | 8 x 5 | 4 x 3 | 3 x 7

10 x 5 | 8 x 2 | 2 x 10 | 2 x 6 | 10 x 3 | 5 x 3 | 4 x 2

 Brilliant Ideas for Times Tables 5–7 © Molly Potter 2012

The 3 x Table

Colour match

Name _____ **Date** _____

Colour the sums in the box different colours. For example 1 x 3 could be black and 2 x 3 could be green etc. Now find the answers and colour them to match.

33   36

3

30   9   21

24

30   18

15

3

27   12

6   12

21   24

9

36

33

18

15   6

27

Find out what they said

Name _____ **Date** _____

Use the table to find out what strange things these creatures said.

3	6	9	12	15	18	21	24	27	30
married	beautiful	car	bite	footballer	deep-sea diver	pet	boxer	home	eat

We have been _____ for ten years. `3 x 1`

It's great as long as he remembers not to _____ me. `3 x 10`

Will you be my _____? `3 x 7`

You are _____. `3 x 2`

OK but I warn you I do _____. `3 x 4`

When I grow up, I want to be a _____ `3 x 6`

I just got a job as a _____ – at least I think that was what it was. `3 x 5`

Does that mean you will have to give up your job as a _____? `3 x 8`

This is a robbery. Hand over your _____. `3 x 9`

Wouldn't you rather have my_____? `3 x 3`

Sue Slug

Sid Snail

What do they eat?

Name _____ **Date** _____

Match the sums to their answers to find out what these monsters, aliens and robots eat. Join them with a pencil, one has been done for you.

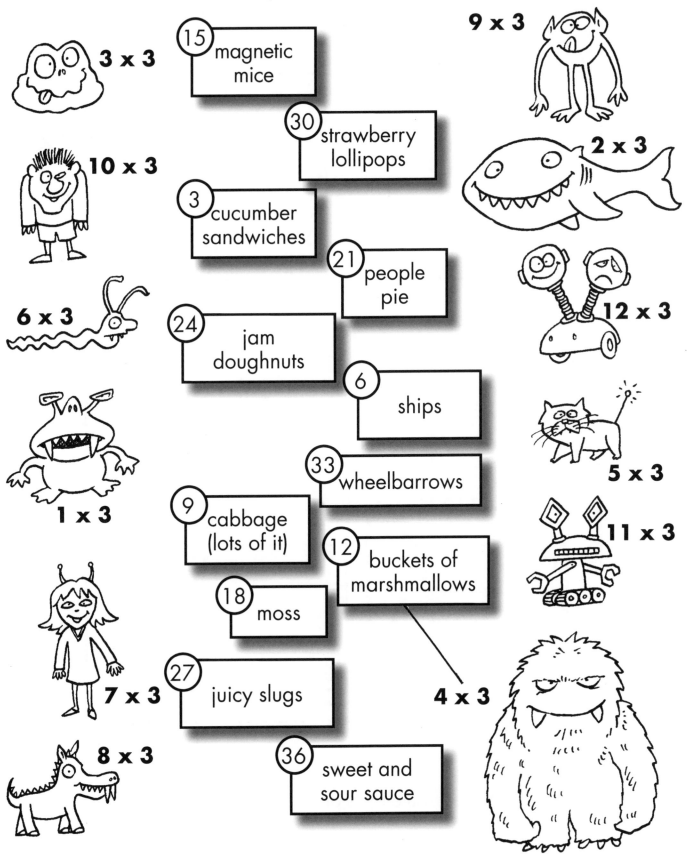

9 x 3

3 x 3   (15) magnetic mice

(30) strawberry lollipops

2 x 3

10 x 3   (3) cucumber sandwiches

(21) people pie

12 x 3

6 x 3   (24) jam doughnuts

(6) ships

(33) wheelbarrows

5 x 3

1 x 3   (9) cabbage (lots of it)

(12) buckets of marshmallows

11 x 3

(18) moss

7 x 3   (27) juicy slugs

4 x 3

8 x 3   (36) sweet and sour sauce

Journey to the answer

Name _____ **Date** _____

Use different colours to show the route each sum would take along the roads to arrive at its answer. You can only travel along the roads and not through the park. One (1 x 3) has been done for you.

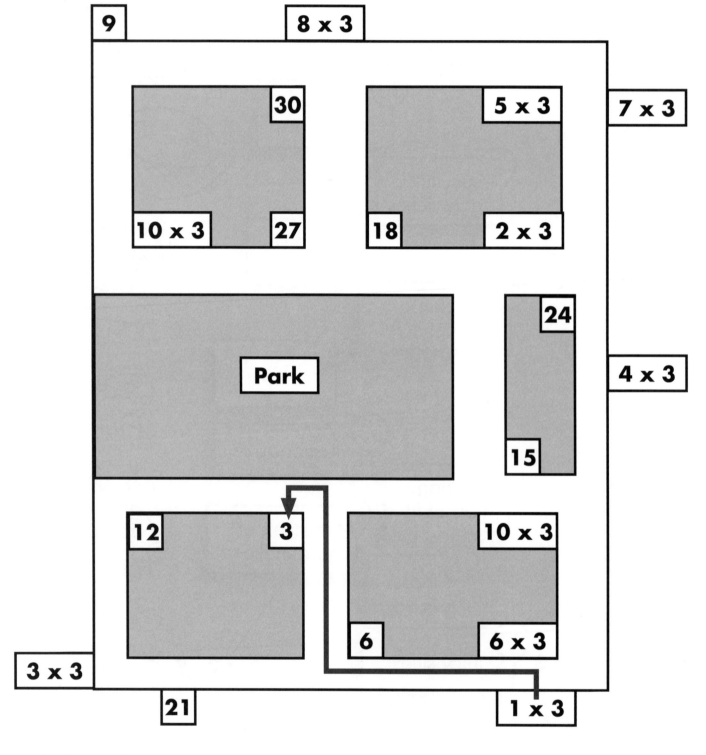

Which sum had the shortest route to its answer?   3 x _____ = _____

Which sum had the longest route to its answer?   3 x _____ = _____

Activity Sheet 44

x3

Label with sums

Name ______________________ **Date** ______________

Find as many things as you can to label with the following sums in this picture. One has been done for you.

1 x 3	**2 x 3**	**3 x 3**	**4 x 3**	**5 x 3**
6 x 3	**7 x 3**	**8 x 3**	**9 x 3**	**10 x 3**

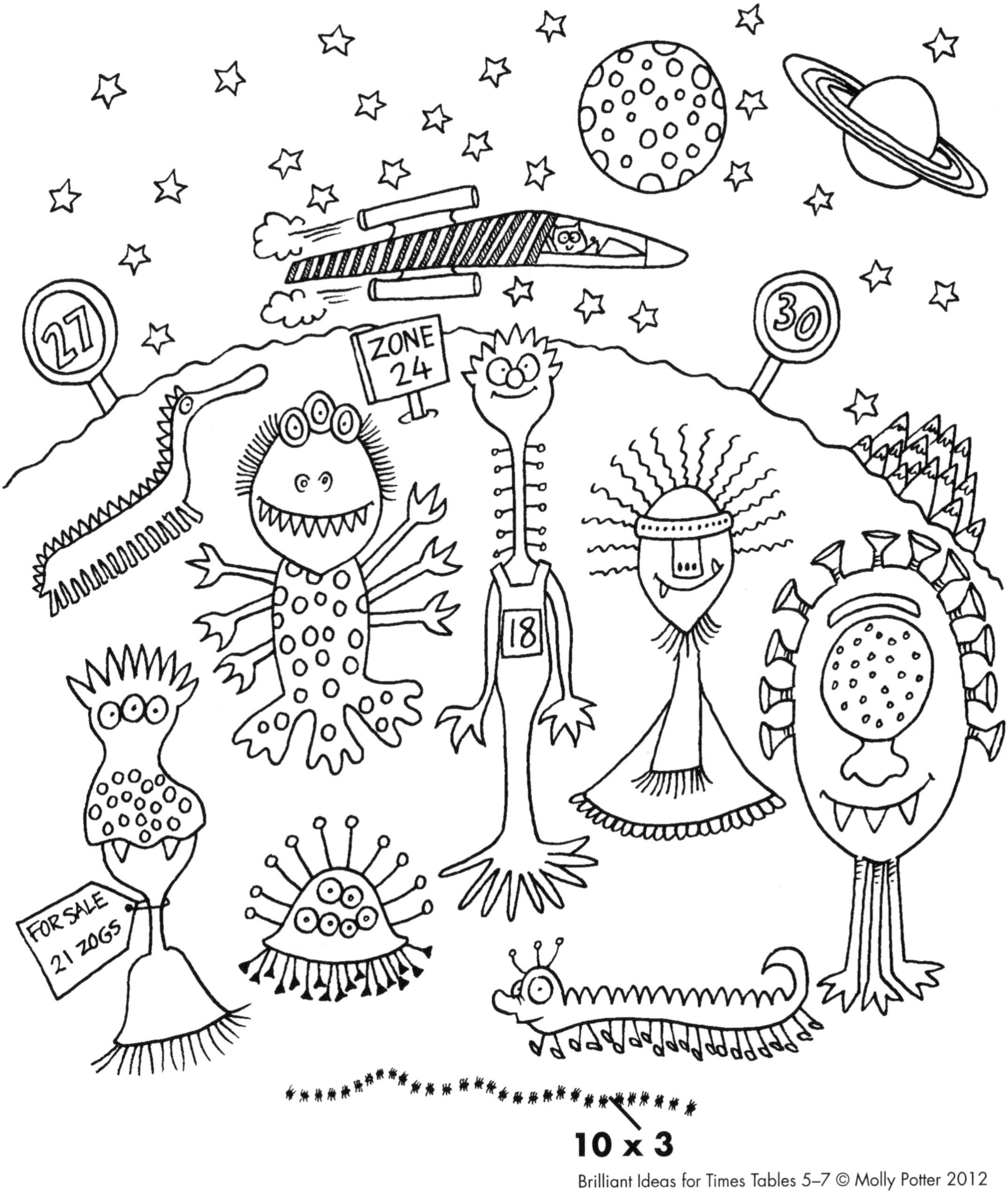
27
30
ZONE 24
18
FOR SALE 21 ZOGS
10 x 3

Complete the picture

Name _____ **Date** _____

This is Igor. He is quite an ugly monster. The problem is, this picture of him has some missing bits. Use the answers to these sums to complete his picture.

3 x 9 spiky hairs on his head

3 x 6 eyelashes in total

3 x 3 hairs on his chin

3 x 7 spots on his face

3 x 1 teeth sticking out

3 x 2 earrings in total

3 x 8 stripes on his jacket

3 x 4 fingers in total

3 x 5 dots on his trousers

He is 3 x 10 = _____ years old.

How many triangles?

Name _____ **Date** _____

Use a ruler to join the sums to their answers with a straight line. Colour in any triangles that are made by the straight lines.

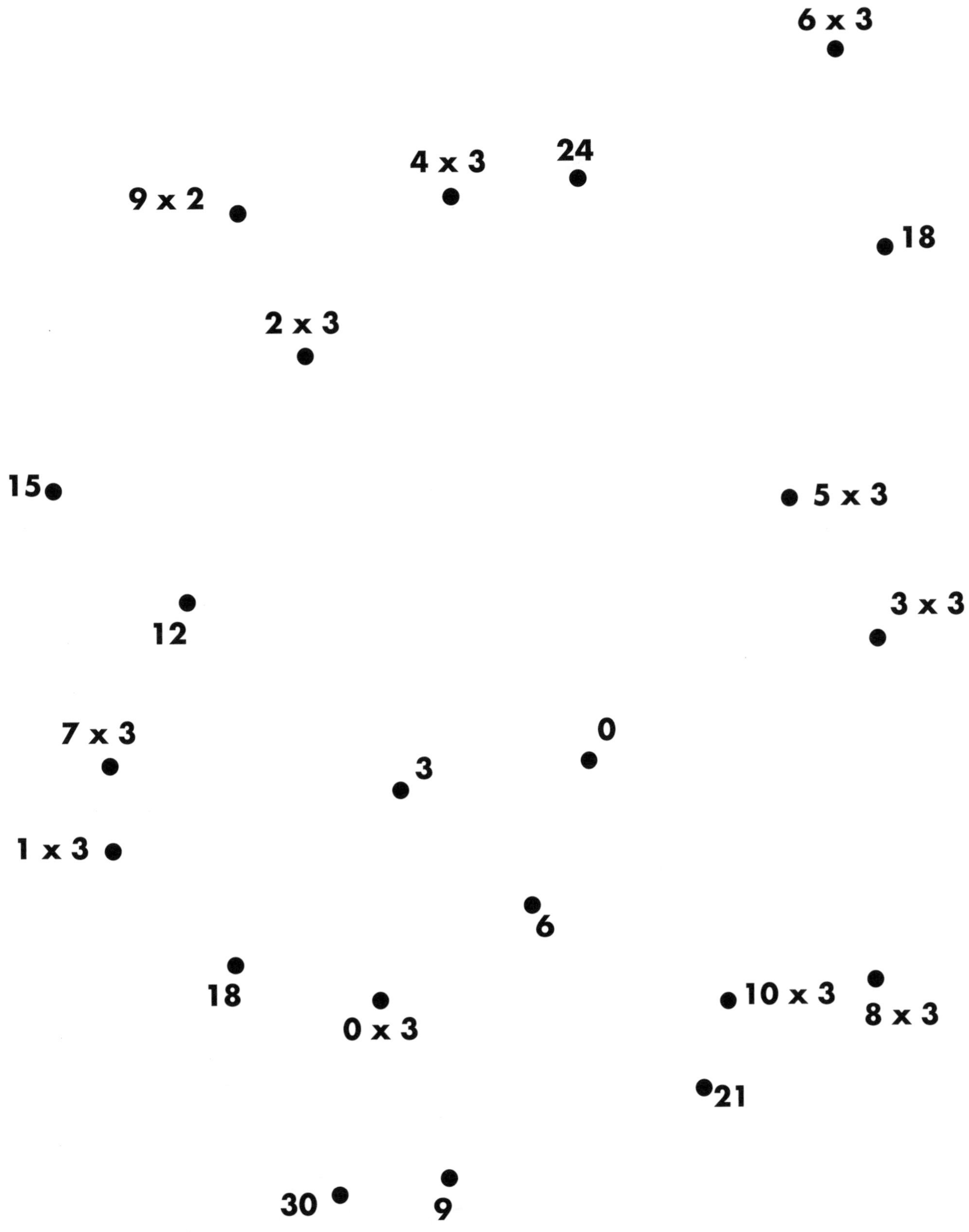

6 x 3 •

4 x 3 •   24 •

9 x 2 •

• 18

2 x 3 •

15 •

• 5 x 3

• 12

3 x 3 •

7 x 3 •   0 •

• 3

1 x 3 •

• 6

• 18

• 0 x 3   • 10 x 3   • 8 x 3

• 21

30 •   • 9

Number of triangles that I made = _____

Monster meal

Name _____ **Date** _____

Graff Greedy the monster only likes food that has been priced an amount that is in the three times table. Draw what he will eat on his plate.

2p

12p

9p

18p

4p

33p

15p

24p

10p

21p

20p

16p

This is the answer: what is the question?

Name _____ **Date** _____

Circle the sum on each line that matches the answers on the left.

9	2 x 3	3 x 3	4 x 3	5 x 3
15	3 x 3	4 x 3	5 x 3	6 x 3
30	7 x 3	8 x 3	9 x 3	10 x 3
3	0 x 3	1 x 3	2 x 3	3 x 3
12	4 x 3	5 x 3	6 x 3	7 x 3
6	1 x 3	2 x 3	3 x 3	4 x 3
18	3 x 3	4 x 3	5 x 3	6 x 3
24	5 x 3	6 x 3	7 x 3	8 x 3
27	7 x 3	8 x 3	9 x 3	10 x 3
21	7 x 3	8 x 3	9 x 3	10 x 3
15	8 x 3	6 x 3	7 x 3	5 x 3
24	7 x 3	9 x 3	8 x 3	6 x 3
21	8 x 3	6 x 3	7 x 3	9 x 3
18	8 x 3	7 x 3	6 x 3	9 x 3
27	9 x 3	6 x 3	7 x 3	8 x 3

x3   **Name** _____   **Date** _____

Race!

Use these two sets of sums to race with a friend. The same sums are in each set but in a different order. You will need to cut the page down the middle.

5 x 3 =	3 x 4 =
2 x 3 =	3 x 2 =
3 x 2 =	7 x 3 =
4 x 3 =	1 x 3 =
3 x 6 =	3 x 9 =
3 x 3 =	8 x 3 =
10 x 3 =	3 x 3 =
3 x 1 =	10 x 3 =
3 x 2 =	3 x 8 =
6 x 3 =	3 x 10 =
3 x 3 =	3 x 1 =
1 x 3 =	2 x 3 =
3 x 5 =	9 x 3 =
7 x 3 =	3 x 6 =
3 x 4 =	4 x 3 =
3 x 9 =	5 x 3 =
8 x 3 =	6 x 3 =
9 x 3 =	3 x 3 =
3 x 7 =	3 x 7 =
3 x 10 =	3 x 5 =

Answers

Answers are not given for activities where these are simply the result of a multiplication sum.

Activity sheet 7:
Whose sum is it?
(2 times table)

Activity sheet 9:
Sum search
(2 times table)

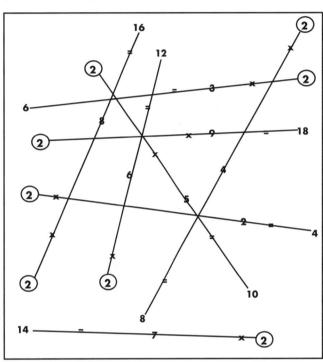

Activity sheet 8:
Hidden numbers
(2 times table)

x 2 multiplication sum	Number of answers
1 x 2	6
2 x 2	4
3 x 2	7
4 x 2	6
5 x 2	3
6 x 2	6
7 x 2	3
8 x 2	3
9 x 2	3
10 x 2	5

Activity sheet 10:
Answer hunt
(2 times table)

Question	Answer
How many clouds are there?	2 x 3
How many hairs come out of the alien's ears?	2 x 9
How many spiky trees are there?	2 x 3
How many fruits are there in the fruit bush?	2 x 9
How many teeth has the alien?	2 x 6
How many wheels on the alien's car?	2 x 5
How many eyes has the alien?	2 x 2
How many spots on the alien's nose?	2 x 7

Activity sheet 16:
Hidden picture
(5 times table)
A witch on a broomstick.

Activity sheet 19:
Dot to dot in fives
(5 times table)

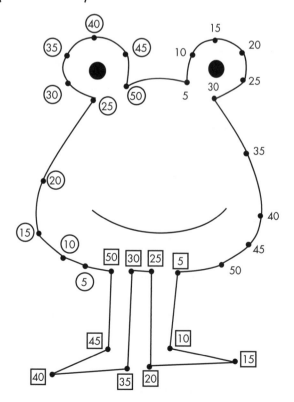

Activity sheet 20:
Treasure Island
(5 times table)
The treasure is in the old oak as the journey makes an arrow that points to it.

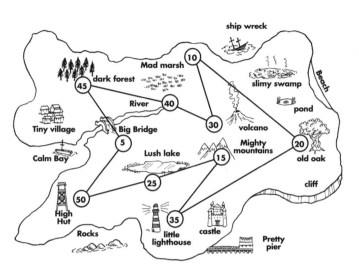

Activity sheet 23:
Get rid of the wrong answers
(10 times table)

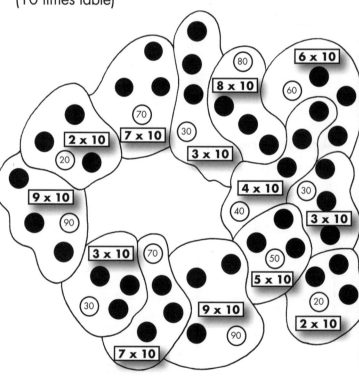

Activity sheet 25:
Who has the most balloons?
(10 times table)
7 x 10 has three balloons.

Brilliant Ideas for Times Tables 5–7 © Molly Potter 2012

Activity sheet 27:
Find out about Trogg
(10 times table)
- slugs
- trolls
- cars
- trees
- cheese

Activity sheet 28:
Find the answers
(10 times tables)

Activity sheet 32:
What's hidden in the picture?
(2, 5 and 10 times tables)
A star.

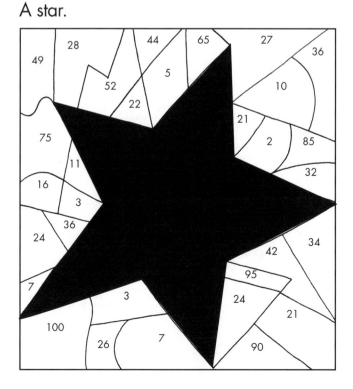

Activity sheet 34:
What is his job?
(2, 5 and 10 times tables)
He is a really strong magnet.

Activity sheet 36:
Which is bigger?
(2, 5 and 10 times tables)

1)	4 x 2	10)	5 x 5
2)	2 x 5	11)	2 x 3
3)	1 x 5	12)	3 x 5
4)	3 x 5	13)	5 x 6 same 3 x 10
5)	2 x 6	14)	9 x 2
6)	2 x 5	15)	5 x 2
7)	8 x 2	16)	3 x 5
8)	7 x 5	17)	4 x 10 same 8 x 5
9)	4 x 5	18)	5 x 5
		19)	1 x 10 same 2 x 5
		20)	2 x 10

Activity sheet 37:
Dot to dot
(2, 5 and 10 times tables)

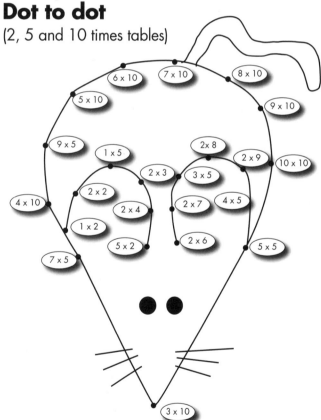

Activity sheet 38:
Monster maths
(2, 5 and 10 times tables)

1.	25	5.	15	9.	50	13.	12
2.	16	6.	60	10.	35	14.	45
3.	100	7.	20	11.	30		
4.	14	8.	70	12.	40		

Activity sheet 39:
Who won the race?

(2, 3, 5 and 10 times tables)
12 won the race.

4	✓	✓				
5	✓	✓				
6	✓					
8	✓					
9	✓					
10	✓					
12	✓	✓	✓	✓	✓	✓
15	✓	✓	✓			
16	✓	✓	✓			
18	✓	✓	✓	✓		
20	✓	✓	✓	✓		
21	✓	✓				
24	✓	✓				
25	✓	✓	✓			
27	✓	✓				
30	✓	✓	✓			
35	✓	✓				
40	✓					
45	✓	✓				
50	✓	✓				

Activity sheet 44:
Label with sums

(3 times table)

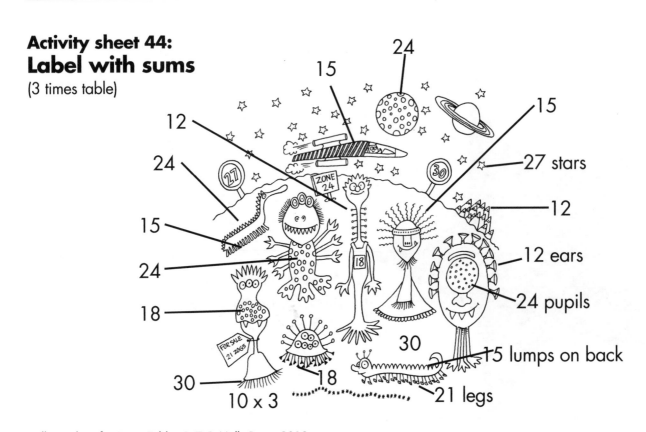

24

15

15

27 stars

12

12 ears

24 pupils

15 lumps on back

21 legs

30

10 x 3

18

30

18

15

24

24

12